ALPHA CHRISTIANS

ALPHA CHRISTIANS

A MANIFESTO FOR MEN

BILL GIOVANNETTI

ISBN (print version): 978-1-946654-30-4

ISBN (ebook): 978-1-946654-31-1

Published in the United States of America.

Printed in the United States on acid free paper.

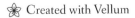 Created with Vellum

Dedicated with gratitude to all the unnamed heroes who have fought for freedom and for truth.

CONTENTS

I live in America. I have the right to write whatever I want. And it's equaled by another right just as powerful: the right not to read it. Freedom of speech includes the freedom to offend people.

~*Brad Thor*

We own the responsibility of calling a culture in
decline, calling the men back.
~*Tony Evans*

I'm not in this world to live up to your expectations and
you're not in this world to live up to mine.
~*Bruce Lee*

A REMARKABLE THING happened in the summer of
2015. A brash, narcissistic, boastful, morally question-
able, politically incorrect outsider announced his
candidacy for President of the United States and
soared to the top of the polls. The pundits were
stunned. How could this politically inexperienced,
offensive outsider, be embraced by so many people?
Why were people drawn to this man?

There were differing opinions on why Donald

Trump experienced his meteoric political rise. One of the prevailing views was that the American public was sick and tired of the politically correct system, the insider politics, and the seemingly never changing landscape of the power brokers in Washington. There was anger. Righteous anger. A huge group of people did not feel their government was working for them.

Along came an Alpha male who spoke to them in plain, unedited, unscripted language. He told it like he saw it. There was no campaign manager advising him to just stick to the script. No words were parsed. It was raw. It was from the gut. It was direct. It was, to half the country, offensive. To the other half, it was a breath of fresh air. But, there was no question as to who was in charge of any speech, any campaign stop, any debate, any discussion. Trump. Donald Trump was the leader. Donald Trump was in charge. Trump was the undeniable Alpha.

Whether you loved or hated him, whether you agreed with him or not, whether he offended you or not, it could not be denied – he was vital, unapologetic, unbending, tough, in charge. Trump equaled Alpha.

No, I'm not upholding Donald Trump as a paragon of Christian virtue. He isn't. In many ways, he is the opposite. I pray for him. I can only imagine the difference he could make if he were completely given over to God.

But today, I submit, we Christians have abdicated our divine calling as Alphas. Where art thou, O Alpha

Christian? Where are the Christians that unabashedly stand for biblical truth and righteousness? Where are the Christian leaders who do not bow to the fads and morality of Hollywood and the cultural elites? Where is some righteous masculinity when we need it?

Where are the Christians who do not sacrifice the clear teachings of the Bible for the murky shallows of politically correct "tolerance?" Where are the church leaders who stand up and say *"Enough!"*? Where are the Christian innovators, creators, producers and leaders? Why are we so often content to sit meekly in the shadows of the secular power-broker elites?

Where is the church that turned the world upside down?

Wake up! Gear up! We need you!

Our country, and indeed our world, is seeing a spectacular decline in morality, in acceptance of absolute truth, and in respect for authority. We are seeing insane acquiescence to violence, rioting, corruption, and doctrinal defection, driven by the Sexual Revolution 2.0 coupled with a laughably revisionist history.

We are seeing a rise in what can only be called a Parasitic Class, determined to suck every drop of blood out of hard working producers and their children and grand children. All of this is rationalized by egg-headed academicians who've never had an idea that actually worked. These in turn are empowered by mercenary politicians gifted with an ability to make the doctrines of demons sound angelic. The whole cabal is backed by a media elite steeped in big-government socialism. And it all works because of a gullible, narcissistic, hypnotized, morally fluid populous hellbent on having a good time.

Don't hassle me, bruh.

Yet, we Christians sit meekly on the sidelines afraid to be noticed, afraid to offend, afraid to anger anyone, when the very foundations of a biblical worldview, and the Western civilization it produced, are being swept away.

Too many so called pastors have swallowed the lie that if they are nice, the world will like them. If we soften our doctrines, our message will be "irresistible" and people will be saved.

Jesus pukes at the thought.

When we will stand up and become the Alphas we should be? I should say that while everything I write applies to both men and women, my main target will be men. And by men I mean those born with male anatomy.

We are not meant to sing love songs to Jesus while the temple of our world is turned into a den of thieves, stealing away life, liberty and the pursuit of happiness.

Without knowing it, the world eagerly awaits a resurgence of Alpha Christians.

This will only happen when we take our stand unapologetically on the plain reading of the Word of God. And that can only happen when the people of God rip off the mask that muzzles us, refusing to to shrink back from the satanic vomit of trigger warnings, critical theories, and irrational mandates.

Let's go men. Let's roll.

By the way, Merry Christmas, God bless America, and see you in church.

WHAT IS AN ALPHA?_

And if you think tough men are dangerous, wait until
you see what weak men are capable of.
~*Jordan B. Peterson*

The ultimate measure of a man is not where he stands
in moments of comfort and convenience, but where he
stands at times of challenge and controversy.
~*Martin Luther King Jr.*

ALPHAS RULE their world for the good of the pack.
Natural born leaders, they may snap and snarl, but
only to put unruly pack members in their place.
Nobody elected them. Nobody anointed them. The
pack just knows. They sense a leader, and they thrive
under the leader's influence.

It's an influence that isn't calculated: it just comes
from the heart.

For the Alpha Christian, it's a heart governed by Christ.

Their creed is the Golden Rule.

Their code is common sense.

Their manifesto is Scripture.

Their motto is "duty with honor at any cost."

Their goal is to know their God.

Their mission is to lead hell-bound neighbors to a saving knowledge of Christ.

Their reward is the smile of the Heavenly Father and the satisfaction of a life well spent.

Their medals are the scars they wear.

Like Jesus, Alphas seek neither approval nor fame. They have a moral compass that isn't up for a vote. For them, some things are right, some things are wrong; there's nothing confusing about it. Alphas leave the endless blathering over moral nuances to their back-stabbing, pencil-pushing, "Beta" counterparts.

WHAT ARE ALPHAS?

Alphas get their work done, and they expect others to do the same.

Alphas do not seek conflict, but they won't back down when conflict is unavoidable.

Alphas love civil conversation and they long to discuss opposing views with mutual respect and maximum empathy.

Alphas respect boundaries; they want to be left

alone, and they're happy to leave others alone... even as...

Alphas help those in need. They protect the pack's weaker members while upholding each one's dignity and insisting all pull their own weight.

Alphas uphold the sacredness of each person as a bearer of the image of God.

Alphas respect other people's property as the hard-won prize of their toil.

Alphas have a powerful sense of justice pulsing within their breasts.

Alphas pay their own way.

Alphas pursue transcendent values without dropping the ball on everyday responsibilities. They're on this planet for themselves, but not only for themselves. There is a mission, a cause, a purpose that rises above changing the oil on their cars, watching their kids' recitals, or hunkering down in sequestered obscurity.

Alphas hate nanny-worship in all its forms, including a nanny-state, a nanny-school, or a nanny-church. They see nanny-intrusion as a tactic of weakling Betas to seize control over oblivious numb-bots.

Alphas embrace their God-given rights of life, liberty, and the pursuit of happiness, believing these rights find their highest expression in Christ.

Alphas believe in free will. They take one hundred percent responsibility for the quality of their life, and they are done making excuses.

Alphas hold themselves responsible for the quality of their lives and expect others to do the same.

Alphas will not go quietly into the night while the world washes down the gutter of satanic infiltration. They will resist to the end, for the sake of their children, their children's children, and for the cause of the gospel in the world.

VARIETY

I am not talking about macho men being macho. Alphas affirm a wide variety of masculine expressions. Real men come in all shapes and sizes, and we all have each other's backs.

Alpha males can be artistic, athletic, academic, macho, rugged, musical, sensitive, caring, witty, mechanical, mathematical, soft, hard, muscular, scrawny, round, financially oriented, entrepreneurial, blue-collar, beer-drinking, wine-sipping, teetotaling, dirty-job-tradesmen, metrosexual, suave, socially awkward, or any other variety you can think of.

Some are into sports, others appreciate the feel of nice fabric, the symphony, or NASCAR. Some admire a gourmet meal at a well-set table. Others would rather chow down campfire beans with a spork.

We don't care.

We all have each other's backs.

Race, ethnicity, color, creed, family of origin, and other inherited factors are interesting—but not determinative. You are the man you have chosen to become, regardless of the cards life dealt you. Have you had it hard? Me too. Quit whining and choose your adventure.

An Alpha Christian is not stupid. Never a jerk. Never a cheater. Not violent unless absolutely necessary. Never abusive. Never demeaning. The moment our Inner Bully is unleashed, our Alpha status evaporates.

At their core, they have respect for themselves, their God, their wives, their families, and their neighbors. They love their country, they pursue righteousness and want to live and let live.

They hate interference in their lives, whether from a petty government bureaucrat, a corporate boardroom bully, a snoopy homeowners association, a tax-and-spend politician, a legalistic pastor, or a discourteous punk down the street blasting his music too loud.

An Alpha is a good man with a good heart, no matter his exterior.

St. Paul spoke to Alphas when he wrote, "Be on the alert, stand firm in the faith, act like men, be strong. Let all that you do be done in love" (1 Corinthians 16:13, 14, NASB).

God roused Alphas with his prewar pep talk to Joshua. "Have I not commanded you? Be strong and of good courage; do not be afraid, nor be dismayed, for the Lord your God is with you wherever you go" (Joshua 1:9).

Jesus warned Alphas to stand strong when he said, "Do not think that I came to bring peace on earth. I did not come to bring peace, but a sword. (Matthew 10:34).

What is an Alpha Christian? A man who loves God, truth, the gospel, family, and patriotism, and who will fight for these values, even if it means he gets a bloody nose or worse.

> - WHAT IS AN ALPHA CHRISTIAN? A MAN WHO LOVES GOD, TRUTH, THE GOSPEL, FAMILY, AND PATRIOTISM, AND WHO WILL FIGHT FOR THESE VALUES, EVEN IF IT MEANS HE GETS A BLOODY NOSE OR WORSE.

POLITICAL?

This whole thing is just a smokescreen to advance right-wing politics, right? Wrong.

We're here to advance the gospel.

Alpha Christians can be found everywhere on today's political spectrum. In fact, we are more likely to view today's political parties as opponents in a World Wrestling match. It looks like they're fighting, but at the end of the day, they're sitting in the same room splitting up the same piles of cash.

We are less interested in politics than in the biblically mandated moral issues that drive them. Alpha Christians speak to moral issues. Where that intersects with politics, what do you want? Do you want us to sit down and shut up?

That's funny.

Everything criticized in this book is a moral issue, first and foremost. Wherever moral evil stretches its tentacles into politics, media, academia, social media, entertainment, culture, government, and our kids' schools, you will find Alphas brandishing the sword of truth to slice and dice the devil's lies.

These lies stand in direct competition to the gospel. They promise their own kind of salvation. They deaden the spiritual quest, harden the conscience, and distract from God.

Our public morality, or lack of it, is a barometer of our collective desire for God. It also defines that desire, sometimes right out of existence.

Our culture urgently needs more Alpha Christians involved in every level of politics and civic discourse.

The deepest moral issue for us is the right of individuals to be themselves, to embrace their dominion, to step into liberty, under the influence of Jesus Christ as Savior and Lord.

Freedom!

This is not about a liberal/conservative, left/right, democrat/republican divide.

It is about individual liberty versus collective tyranny, and whether we bow the knee to Christ or to "the party."

No, the needs of the many do not outweigh the

needs of the one. No, I am not my brother's keeper, and my brother is not my keeper—back off—you're not my brother, anyway. No, we do not believe "from each according to his ability, to each according to his needs." These big-government socialist slogans are verbal wolves in sheep's clothing. They trample individualism and property rights in the name of "the greater good," a good which is always defined by elites who—with the help of useful idiots—enrich themselves to their own damnation.

No, the early church did not practice communism or anything like it. What they did was voluntary and had nothing to do with government coercion. No, the Bible did not mandate giving handouts through its policy of gleaning. Hungry people had to go out and actually work for their lunch—more like workfare than welfare.

God spare us from do-gooders determined to help others at someone else's expense.

St. Paul warned that Satan himself appears as an angel of light. Our entire culture has fallen for this con, but Alpha Christians haven't; we see the devil's hollow glare peering back at us.

Bring back rugged individualism.

The minute any group tries to foist Marxism, big-government socialism, communism, fascism, or Nazism upon an unwitting populace, Alpha Christians will take our stand on Scripture, which stands for private property, liberty, and the individual. If that makes us political, that's what you get for waking a sleeping giant.

The gospel flows wherever freedom of thought, speech, and choice flow. We fight for freedom, ultimately, so that our neighbors and our world might hear of the Savior.

You can be an Alpha Christian and vote for a democrat, a republican, a libertarian, or a green. All these platforms are tainted anyway—it's just a matter of degree. We suffer political homelessness—we're holding our nose no matter who gets our vote.

Wherever you find yourself politically, fight for freedom and we'll be on your side.

Above all, our loyalty is to Jesus, his gospel, and his Word. We respect the ideals of our nation, but we do not make an idol of it. After Jesus, we prioritize our liberty, our marriage, our family, and a civil society that protects individuals and their property from the greed of morally empty collectivists and corporatists. These things unite us.

Other than that, you leave us alone, and we'll leave you alone—hopefully to mull over your need of salvation. That's a political theory we can all get behind.

Get thee behind me, Satan.
~Jesus

Let us not glide through this world and then slip
quietly into heaven, without having blown the trumpet
loud and long for our Redeemer, Jesus Christ. Let us
see to it that the devil will hold a thanksgiving service
in hell, when he gets the news of our departure from
the field of battle.
~C.T. Studd, athlete turned missionary

JESUS CHRIST RISES head and shoulders above all
others as the Alpha Prime.

No one commanded a room like him. He was and
is a walking, talking force of nature. Tough and tender.
Savage and fierce. Uncontrollable. Nobody tamed him.
Nobody set the agenda for him. Jesus stands unchal-

lenged as the Leader of the Pack, the ultimate Alpha. Far above any sentimental, feminized, wimpy Beta delusions piled on him, there never has been and never will be anyone as Alpha as Jesus.

He didn't wear a dress. He was born a helpless baby but didn't stay that way.

Jesus shocked people. Matthew says Jesus gave a speech, and the crowds were "amazed" at his speaking and "authority." "Everyone was astonished..." (Matthew 7:28,29).

When the religious thugs sent their goons to arrest him, they intended to take him, "but no one laid hands on him" (John 7:44). When their angry bosses demanded an explanation, the cops said, "No man ever spoke like this Man" (v. 46).

Jesus was so Alpha that everyone else, by comparison, was Beta.

His speech was Alpha-speech: direct, pointed, and blunt. He never hesitated to get in someone's face when they needed it. Jesus rebuked his disciples for being stupid, foolish, and dimwitted. When one disciple asked Jesus a nosy question, Jesus told him it was none of his business: "What is that to you?" (John 21:22).

He called the religious thugs fools. He openly mocked their pomposity. He blasted them as "a brood of vipers" and "child[ren] of Hell" (Luke 3:7, Matthew 23:15).

Like all Alphas, Jesus spoke plainly. He didn't

mince words. Never flattered. Never softened the blow with endless qualifiers and disclaimers. He spoke the truth in love. He spoke with emotion, but never let emotion run amok. He never abused, never slandered, and never mistreated anyone. For him, truth was spoken in love, and truth was an absolute defense.

Did he sound harsh at times? Did he step on toes? So what? For him, stern language was the only scalpel sharp enough to slice through the thick callous of lies deadening his listeners' hearts.

How would Jesus fare in today's churches? In an age of flattery and fluff, who would put up with him? Most would turn away. He triggered everybody. "He's unloving," they would say. "Such a bully. So rude!"

Jesus was a micro-aggression waiting to happen.

And so, the Beta-fied Christian wimps would slink over to whatever church would suckle their narcissistic egos and soothe their jittery emotions.

As an Alpha, Jesus was supremely rational. He spoke with blistering confidence because he spoke irrefutable truth. When the Pharisees tried to trap him, Jesus trapped them back. When they tried to out-Scripture him, he double out-Scriptured them to the point where they picked up stones to kill him. With Satan at his finest, and Jesus at his weakest, Jesus still embarrassed him by logic, Scripture, theology, and mental toughness.

Poor stupid devil. He'd never faced an Alpha in human skin before.

Jesus didn't preface his speech with disclaimers. He saw no need to issue qualifiers or exceptions. If the truth offended, so be it. If it hurt, he knew it would eventually heal. There was not one molecule of political correctness in his being.

The Alpha Prime also spoke with supreme tenderness. When the religious thugs dragged a woman from her bed of adultery and threw her at Jesus' feet for judgment, Jesus called her "Woman" (John 8:10). He was the first one to treat her as a person instead of an object. For Jesus, calling her "Woman" was a sign of respect. A mark of dignity. A statement of affection. From his bloody Cross, he spoke to his mother the same word, committing her into the hands of his friend, John: "Woman, behold your son..." (John 19:26).

Whether embracing children, comforting the bereaved, healing the sick, giving sight to the blind, causing the lame to walk, or giving advice on how to fish, Jesus comforted the afflicted and afflicted the comforted as the situation required.

Christian—the man you follow is a man's man. He looked, smelled, walked, and talked like an Alpha. He didn't slouch around. And he never apologized for a syllable that crossed his lips, because he didn't have to. He had the wisdom to tailor his words for maximum impact on those who were teachable. He had the righteous indignation to blast the arrogant know-it-alls as the fools they were.

Life is a storm, my young friend. You will bask in the sunlight one moment, be shattered on the rocks the next. What makes you a man is what you do when that storm comes. You must look into that storm and shout as you did in Rome. "Do your worst, for I will do mine!"
~*The Count of Monte Cristo*

Then He arose and rebuked the wind, and said to the sea, "Peace, be still!" And the wind ceased and there was a great calm. But He said to them, "Why are you so fearful? How is it that you have no faith?"
~*The Gospel of Mark*

A CARPENTER IN JESUS' day did not have the luxury of running to Home Depot for a load of two-by-fours. He had to fell the tree and produce the lumber.

Today's carpenters specialize: rough carpenter, trim carpenter, cabinet-maker, house framer, ship's carpenter. Not so with Jesus. He was a jack-of-all-trades.

Whatever toughness and skill come to your mind when you hear the word *carpenter*, double it for Jesus.

Jesus would have learned the trade from his stepfather, Joseph. Jesus was Joseph's apprentice. Joseph taught Jesus how to use the tools of the trade, how to design and build furniture, vessels, boxes, and buildings.

For tools, Jesus would have used a rough ribbon as a saw. He would have used an awl instead of a drill. For a hammer, he would use a rock. And for lumber, he would start with a rough-hewn log. Jesus built what he built without a table saw, a planer, jointer, lathe, scroll saw, band saw, or sandpaper.

He was physically tough and mentally alert. He was a muscular, hard-working man. His hands were calloused and cut with the scars of the trade.

At age fifteen, Jesus would have taken over the family business. This was a necessity because scholars think Joseph died early in the life of Jesus. For the next fifteen years, he perfected his skills as a carpenter.

Strong, smart, hardworking—he was a man whose hands were calloused by rough work.

One time, after Jesus shocked his listeners with his biblical teaching, the people scratched their heads and said, "Isn't this the carpenter?" (Mark 6:3). Mike Rowe could do an episode on him.

Jesus gives dignity to every hard-working man and woman today. Whether you swing a hammer, drive a truck, dig a ditch, change a diaper, or scrub a floor, Jesus has been there with you. Don't ever think that you need a religious job to serve God.

Alpha Christians relish the idea of dirty jobs if they know the work will make a difference—and making a difference includes paying the bills.

Being an Alpha Christian doesn't require that you work with your hands; that's irrelevant. It makes no difference whether you wear a suit and tie, coveralls, apron, sweatpants, or a lab coat. What matters is that you take pride in your vocation and never feel diminished by it, no matter how humble. For an Alpha, there is no such thing as menial work. If it's honest labor, it's dignifying enough. In the home. Outside the home. In the boardroom. Out on the back forty. Latest fashion statements. Torn blue jeans. Alpha Christians couldn't care less about a person's outward trappings.

They respect work. They honor any and all who refuse to live by the sweat of another person's brow.

Their blood boils at the thought of parasitic takers.

Can you be hip without being pretentious? Perfect. Sport your cuffed skinny jeans and hipster fedora without checking every mirror you pass. Can you be cool but not cocky? Upper class but not snooty? Can you be a redneck, pickup truck, flannel-shirt tough guy without sneering at the metrosexual who just stumbled into the bar? Be what you are and let others be what they are. The Alpha Christian's ethic of hard work and fair play has created in them a healthy respect for every person's liberties and rights.

Those who reach Alpha status feel no need to point it out. Jesus never said, "I'm in charge here." He walked softly and carried a big stick. If he boasted, he boasted in his Father. He mixed with rich people and poor people, children and beggars, clean and pure or messed up and fallen. He was a friend of anyone who would be a friend of his.

Alphas don't put on airs. Jesus was the celebrity of the universe, but he lived in obscurity. He was the Quiet Man.

But there was that time he overturned tables in the Temple. He saw the greed, the lies, the outright theft. He saw the preachers using religious laws to fleece the flock. His anger burned red hot. He made a whip. Think about that. He's grabbing leather, winding, weaving, sputtering, fuming. He's swinging at everyone in sight. Get out! Get out! Stop it! You've made my Father's house a den of thieves!

He's flipping over tables. Spilling piles of ill-gotten money. Breaking turtle-doves out of their cages to let them fly away.

He's raising welts on pale-skinned priests and pudgy-handed religionists who never did an honest day's work in their lives. He crashed their crooked party, and he showed them up as the cowards they've always been.

Jesus gained nothing for himself by this ultimate Alpha display.

He was all about the glory of God.

Most churches would kick him out. Because most churches have bought the devil's lie that church is for weak-willed numb-bots who can't handle the truth.

What is truth?

Hard, exacting, tough, uncompromising reality, as revealed by God. And a bona fide Alpha Christian burns red hot when puny humans arrogantly trample God's truth.

The pack can't be at peace without its Alpha firmly in place.

"You would have no power over me at all unless it were given you from above," he told Pilate.

Even when bound before kings, Jesus never let there be any doubt about just who was in charge.

THE CONSPIRACY_

If sinners be damned, at least let them leap to Hell over
our dead bodies. And if they perish, let them perish
with our arms wrapped about their knees, imploring
them to stay. If Hell must be filled, let it be filled in the
teeth of our exertions, and let not one go unwarned and
unprayed for.
~*Charles H. Spurgeon*

What important truth do very few people agree with
you on?
~*Peter Thiel*

Alpha Christians are tuned in to the real
conspiracy running the world.

Your thoughts might run to the Illuminati, Bilder-
berg Group, Council on Foreign Relations, United

Nations, George Soros, Bill Gates, and a host of murky entities.

Alpha Christians express a variety of opinions on these theories. Some embrace them, others do not. Alphas respect differing opinions.

But as Christians, there is one Grand Conspirator on whom we all can agree.

Satan.

God gave Adam and Eve dominion. "Go be Alphas," he said. "Wield the scepter of power."

A minute later, they handed the scepter of power to the Serpent, and the world has been going to hell in a handbasket ever since.

St. John explains, "The whole world"—meaning the systems, philosophies, and values of this fallen world—"lies under the sway of the Wicked One" (1 John 5:19).

Jesus called Satan "the Ruler of this world" (John 14:30)

Paul called him "the god of this age" (2 Corinthians 4:4).

In the Temptation, Satan transported Jesus to the top of a high mountain. In a flash, he showed Jesus "all the kingdoms of this world and their glory."

The devil made an offer. "All these things I will give you if you will fall down and worship me."

Jesus took the offer seriously. He didn't laugh it off. He didn't for a moment deny Satan's authority over "all the kingdoms of this world and their glory." He knew who held the scepter.

Jesus had the inner strength to reject the offer. "Away with you, Satan! For it is written, 'You shall worship the Lord your God, and him only shall you serve'" (Matthew 4:8-10).

Satan left him.

But the offer was still on the table. The rights to the world system were signed over to Satan when the original humans threw away their Alpha crowns. Since then, it's the devil's world, the *cosmos diabolicus*.

How does this play out?

It plays out when universities that should be bastions of free thought and debate cancel speakers whose views don't capitulate to the demands of aggrieved snowflakes.

It plays out when the Bible is discarded while every category of deviant literature is foisted on students in modern academia.

It plays out when boys and girls are taught there are 37 genders.

It plays out when corporate elitists make backroom deals with corrupt politicians-for-hire.

It plays out when Hollywood movies hyper-sexualize our youth, foster fornication, normalize same-sex attraction, and celebrate adultery.

It plays out when a biological male enters a women's power-lifting competition and takes home the gold.[1]

It plays out every time politicians assert their own warped view of "doing the right thing" over the Constitution and the law.

It plays out when multi-national businesses maximize profits on the backs of children and their mothers in sweatshops around the world.

It plays out when "social justice" criminals bash in windows and steal big-screen TVs as reparations for past injustice.

It plays out when, on the street, people shout, "Black lives matter" or "Blue lives matter" or "All lives matter," but in the alleys, they cry, "pre-born lives don't matter" and abort them as fast as they can be conceived.

It plays out when anyone justifies racism, anti-Semitism, or sexism by any twisted logic or contorted theology.

It plays out when crosses are dismantled from public squares even as the "Pride" flag is flown at the Department of Interior on Flag Day and over the former US Embassy in Kabul, Afghanistan, as if that is our supreme message to the world.

It plays out when Christians prejudge brothers and sisters who wrestle with sexual confusion—often the result of trauma—and make the church an unsafe place for their struggle.

It plays out when a judicially activist Supreme Court narrowly crams same-sex marriage down the national throat, contravening every piece of legislation that had been passed to date.

It plays out when Twitter, Facebook, social media, and media censor into oblivion traditional values of marriage, family, and patriotism.

It plays out by canceling any view that opposes the mainstream narrative.

It plays out when politicians on both the left and right spew lies to get into office and then conspire to keep themselves in power forever.

It plays out when, in the name of fighting evil, cities defund their police, the primary institution created to fight evil.

It plays out when Churches spew forth emotional-istic, insipid, ultra-tolerant platitudes in the place of hard, tough, exacting doctrine.

It plays out when diversity, inclusion, and equity are weaponized for political ends.

It plays out in anti-Christian bigotry and the illog-ical inversion of the idea of separation of church and state.

It plays out in the war on boys and the demoniza-tion of men.

It plays out in the objectification of girls and the disrespect of women.

It plays out when a male athlete bares his genitalia in a high school women's locker room and our daugh-ters are supposed to accept this crap.

What is going on?

Mass hypnosis.

The devil has hypnotized the whole world. The doctrines of demons have cast their spell. Not to be left behind, academicians have woven webs of verbal sorcery to cloak Luciferian lies in respectable academic garb. Critical race theory. Intersectionality. Systemic racism, sexism, homophobia, and heteronormativity. Cis-gendered. Transgendered. White privilege. Western hegemony. The devil's acid rain is falling so fast no one can keep up with it.

Satan is tricky enough to make Sauron look like a Sunday school teacher. He is clever enough to make a monster look like a Hollywood superstar. He is cunning enough to seduce gullible multitudes. And he is vicious enough to rip your heart out and squeeze the blood over his Fruity Pebbles for breakfast.

He does it all with a smile, a pat on the back, and a barbed hook in your lower lip.

Satan hates the nation-state. He spits on patriotism at every turn. He calls it "nationalism" to tie the love of country to both idol-worship and the Nazis. He wants to prove himself Master of the World, the diabolical replacement messiah. To this end, he is the first global-ist. He must create his one-world government with his one-world religion to bring about his utopian vision, and to fulfill his unhinged dream "to be *like* the Most High" (Isaiah 7:14). Like God. Not unlike God.

Alpha Christians are patriotic. They see sovereign nations as watertight bulkheads on a submarine. If one compartment floods, the whole ship won't go down. If the devil has his way, he'll obliterate those bulkheads—he'll bring about his globalist vision—and flood the whole thing into his waiting arms.

He's even minted the term Christian Nationalism as a pejorative to slap on anybody who loves God and America. As Alphas, we'll call ourselves patriots, and you can call us whatever you like.

Meanwhile, churches are transmogrified into social hubs, pursuing worldly good at the expense of heavenly reward, watering down their doctrines, and singing love songs to Jesus. Never mind getting people saved. Never mind preaching the old, rugged Cross. Never mind teaching the deep things of theology and forming a Christian mind in the minds of Christians. Never mind wearing out our Bibles. Let's just "love on" each other, theology be damned.

It takes an Alpha Christian to push back.

It's time to rise up and call these things what they really are. They are evil because they are irrational.

THAT'S CRAZY

It's not just stupid. It's not just crazy. It's not just nonsensical, incoherent, and contradictory.

It's evil.

Alphas call things as they are.

Irrationality is evil. It is too kind to say that it is just uninformed, or stupid, or senseless. Irrationality is, in fact, the essence of evil. It is the unreality of demonic lies battering themselves against the bedrock laws of our eternal God.

Irrationality is evil's excrement.

It's everywhere. Don't step in it. You'll find especially large piles of it in secular universities and centers of political power. You'll also find it liberally strewn across every social media platform you can name.

Irrationality is the devil's calling card. Sin is irrational. A coup against heaven is irrational. A wolf dressed in sheep's clothing is irrational.

This fallen world is the devil's toilet.

Alpha Christians, get up, roll up your sleeves, and do a deep clean. Start with your own heart. Work out from there.

Alphas have developed the mature skill of *looking beneath the surface*. The Bible calls this *discernment*. Without it, our whole culture, and even our churches, will be sucked into the inescapable whirlpool of the devil's flush.

Do not love the world or the things in the world. If anyone loves the world, the love of the Father is not in him. (1 John 2:15)

Adulterers and adulteresses! Do you not know that friendship with the world is enmity with God?

> Whoever therefore wants to be a friend of the world makes himself an enemy of God. (James 4:4)

Alphas know an open secret. There are invisible, eternal forces locked in an ages-long conflict for the souls of humans and the destiny of the world. The world system distorts every human institution, structure, government, and organization it touches. Media, social media, arts, government, education, academia, entertainment, politics, even sports, and sad to say, even so much that goes on in the church—it's all drunk driving under the influence of Satan. It is mesmerized by the high-sounding nonsense of satanic philosophy.

This is the conspiracy we must fight.

We are fighting for souls. For our lives. For our children and children's children. For our neighbors. For the vulnerable. We are fighting for the glory of God and the name of our Lord Jesus Christ.

FALSE RELIGION

According to the prophets of Scripture, before the return of the Lord, we are to expect a coming world religion, complete with false priests, and a false salvation. As Alpha Christians, we declare war.

The False Priests are the elites of academia, social media, politics, theology, and entertainment. They are thought-police, pulling the levers at the "Ministry of

Truth," and punishing dissent with exile, deplatforming, and loss of personhood.

These priests of Molech have even given themselves a name. They call themselves "the Brights." As in bright lights. There are articles about them:

- "A Bright New World," in *Psychology Today*
- "A Brights Idea," in the *St Petersburg Times*
- "Let There Be Brights," by atheist Richard Dawkins in *Wired Magazine*
- "The Bright Stuff," by atheist Daniel Dennett, in the *New York Times*
- "The World Is in Need of Influential Brights," by atheist *Florian Aigner*

The Brights are priests of a New World Order, a *kosmos* saturated with great ideas that have never actually worked anywhere. They are parasites.

They peddle a false salvation of wokeness, the corporate-government complex, big-government socialism, racism, legalism, social justice, liberation theology, climate justice, globalism, anti-patriotism, "scientific consensus," and sexual liberation.

This is nothing but a mashup of Marxist tyranny and Orwellian doublespeak.

They're not woke. They're in a trance.

It's not social justice. It's injustice leading to social chaos.

It's a theology that can't liberate because it can't set a heart free from the dominion of sin.

For the elites, the real agenda isn't diversity, inclusion, and equity. The real agenda is raw power and wealth. The real agenda is control.

Satan hooked up with the "Rulers of the Age" and birthed a horrible offspring. They named it the New World Order. This spawn of Satan is a leech. It feeds on one thing—human dominion and freedom. It will gleefully suck its host dry.

It's a false religion.

Alphas hate this thing with a vengeance. It is brainwashing our children. It is shackling our speech. It is devouring our generational wealth. Its tentacles reach everywhere. It has no morals. It offers no hope. Beneath its alluring surface, it is a gray pit of despair and damnation.

This is the conspiracy. This is the devil's endgame. This is the war we are in.

But Alphas face this truth war with determination and grit. It is winnable.

God is not worried. He is on his throne. When the rulers of the earth seek to cast him off, he laughs at them. He has imbued us with his great strength. So, taking our stand on the victory of our crucified and risen Savior, we push back the lies, confident in

Christus Victor, the champion we need for the battle of our lives.

> For the weapons of our warfare are not carnal but mighty in God for pulling down strongholds, casting down arguments and every high thing that exalts itself against the knowledge of God, bringing every thought into captivity to the obedience of Christ. ~2 Corinthians 10:4, 5

THE GENTLEMAN BARBARIAN_

This is your life. Be bold with it. Live it with energy and purpose in the direction that excites you. Listen to your heart, look for your dreams: they are God-inspired.
~*Bear Grylls*

I don't have a lot of time for whining... Because when I bring Jesus Christ into the equation, I've changed the story.
~*Tony Evans*

DAVID MURROW'S 2005 BOOK, *Why Men Hate Going to Church*,[1] put into words how Christians all but suffocated the Alpha spirit among Christian men. The church highlighted virtues such as gentleness and caring, and it classified fisticuffs and indeed almost all sports, as ungodly. The music shifted from epic hymns with deep theological lyrics to romance songs for God. Pastors began to speak of "intimacy with Jesus."

No thank you.

Murrow was right. And the message is still clear today.

Good Christian men don't cuss, smell from BO, drink beer, play cards, go to boxing matches, scratch their crotch, or study martial arts. Pro football, being on Sunday morning, became the church's sworn enemy. Worship music was sentimentalized. The blood-red meat of theology was turned into quiche. Languid pastors routinely ordered congregations to "hold hands with their neighbor" for whatever God-awful reasons might inspire them. Denominations erased *Onward Christian Soldiers* from their hymnals and substituted *There's a Sweet, Sweet Spirit in This Place*. Violence was inexcusable. Pacifism ran the show. And the only thing that required a real man was the sacrament of filling the giant coffee urn with water.

To make matters worse, sensitive Christians were now expected to lift their hands in the air and sway to the music. Eyes at half-mast, lips frozen in a grimace of enraptured sweetness, numbingly repetitious lyrics melting neurons by the minute—all of this served as prelude to inoffensive sermons overflowing with appeals to emotion and Twitter-sized non-sequiturs.

Picture Satan laughing, God fashioning thunder-bolts, and Alpha Christians either out on the lake or at home cleaning the septic system. Anything beats the estrogen-fest called church.

Some women might have loved it, but the only males left standing were Betas, and most of them filled the pulpits. Any boy growing up with a normal level of testosterone would get the heck out of church as soon as Mom could no longer drag him there.

By the late 1900s, church attendance stood at 75% female. Any questions?

ALPHA CHRISTIANS WANT GOD

Of course, the church blamed the victims. They said that Alphas were less interested in God. They said that men were not as spiritual. They condemned men for not attending an optional event that routinely condemned men.

Alpha Christians actually want God. They want Jesus. They want theology. They want Bible study. They want red meat. They just don't want churches that are all soft all the time.

Regardless of what they say on the website, the actual mission of a feminized church is church. Relationships. Connections. "We all love each other here. If we have that, we've done our job," they say.

Alpha Christians say otherwise. Give us an enemy. Give us a battle to fight. Give us a mission worth us getting bloodied and bruised. Give us a truth strong enough to hammer into oblivion the lies of Satan. Give us a message that will set captives free. Yes, we are a family, but we are an army too. What's our mission?

We're ready for a fight.

Equip us and send us out. Let's go!

Give us music that actually means something, and put some energy into it. Have fun with it. Enough of this middle-of-the-road soft stuff. Give us classic hymns. Give us a pipe organ that rumbles the chest. Give us some old-fashioned rock 'n' roll. Gospel music. Country music. Anything but this weird hybrid of undefinable softness that is today's wussified worship music.

Give us sermons that teach the Bible. Give us theology. Greek words. Hebrew words. Stretch our minds. Challenge our preconceptions. Dismantle our misconceptions. Construct in us the mind of Christ. Alphas are tired of the world's lies. Don't bring them into church. And don't treat us like dummies. Any man who can break down a carburetor can handle anything theology has to say. Just be logical. Be sequential. And prove what you say with specific Bible verses.

Give us truths that break our addictions. Call us to spiritual maturity. Call us to rise up to the stature of Christ. We hate the dark side within us. We hate the cruelty in us. We hate the self-serving narcissism and self-indulgence we find in ourselves. Show us a redemptive power that can explode those lies and make us the men we long to be. Show us a love that transcends emotions and summons forth a muscular virtue that can grow only as we leave childish things behind.

Give us ministries that target lost people. And while you're at it, acknowledge that some people are lost and some people are saved, and that people who are lost will spend eternity in hell. Don't water that down. Give it to us straight. We want to know that the war we're in matters.

Give us Jesus. Not the pale-faced Jesus who wore dresses and whose face showed signs of digestive disorders.

Give us the Jesus who swung a hammer. Give us the Jesus who tipped over tables. Above all, give us the Jesus who was nailed to a cross yet never once complained and never once felt sorry for himself. Give us a Jesus whose death meant something, and tell us precisely what it meant. Give us a Jesus who shattered the grave and kicked the devil in the teeth. Give us Jesus bloodied but unbowed, and we will follow him to hell and back.

TOXIC MASCULINITY

The term "toxic masculinity" has been weaponized in an attempt to bludgeon holy masculinity out of existence. There is a war on men and boys, and it doesn't come from heaven.

When is masculinity toxic?

Some mental health experts describe toxic

masculinity in terms of *"toughness, anti-feminity*, and *power*."[2] Everything depends on definitions. In and of themselves, both *toughness* and *power* are morally neutral. "Anti-feminity" is its own contradiction. Anyone who denies even the categories of masculine and feminine doesn't get to whine about being anti-one of them.

If *toughness* means the willingness to take a hit and give a righteous one when needed, then Alphas are shamelessly tough. But if toughness means being emotionally calloused or needlessly aggressive, no thanks. To say that toughness is toxic is to either mis-define the word or to slaughter the warrior spirit in men. If it weren't for tough men, the authors who write their anti-tough-men crap wouldn't have the freedom to write it.

Ditto for *"anti-feminity."* Who knew that word existed? Agreed, if men or boys pick on men or boys who are sensitive, artistic, or not traditionally macho, that truly is toxic behavior, and Alpha Christians want nothing to do with it. We hate bullying. We refuse stereotyping. But men aren't women. And women aren't men. There is masculine. There is feminine. There is a spectrum of characteristics. It's all good. Quit labeling as toxic the spirit that dodges bullets to keep you free.

Power itself is never a problem. The abuse of power is the problem; it is always toxic. Alpha Christians stand against abuse, neglect, and mind games. We hate passive-aggressiveness in bosses and employees. We hate it when pastors berate their congregations and when congregations chew up and spit out their pastors. We hate cruelty, abuse, and exploitation. Alphas call the abuse of power toxic and declare war against it, whether exerted by male bullies, female bullies, social media bullies, corporatist bullies, big-government socialist bullies, or the government's bureaucratic bullies.

Power is God's gift. Alphas exercise power in the holy pursuit of holy desires. We will not apologize for our God-given dominion. We want what we want. Alphas hope you feel the same way about yourself. If you don't, what are you going to do about it? We'll help you if you choose. Quit labeling Alphas as toxic just because we refuse to shrink ourselves so you can feel big.

Yes, we want what we want, but it's okay for us to not get what we want. That's life. The mark of a gentlemen is how he reacts when he hears the word No. We're okay with not getting our way. But we will still use our power in holy ways to go after it, and if you're too wimpy to do the same, own it.

Alphas always couple power with respect for the sacredness of persons.

It is toxic to invade another person. It is toxic to transgress boundaries. It is toxic to trample rights. It is toxic to violate body, soul, or spirit.

Power is toxic when power does evil. Just being powerful doesn't make masculinity toxic.

What's flushing our culture down the toilet isn't toxic masculinity, it's *toxic humanity*—infected with sin and dominated by Satan, distorting both women and men.

What's killing us is *toxic secularity*, because to erase God is to obliterate human dignity and to enshrine the survival of the fittest as the only moral code left standing.

The American Psychological Association tips its politically correct hand by proclaiming, "traditional masculinity is psychologically harmful."[3] That's the kind of headline that empowers the Betas to twist satanic power to shred any remaining fragments of decency in society. These liars wouldn't stop at slapping the "toxic masculinity" label on Jesus himself.

There's a deficit of masculinity in American society today.

Let's fix that.

PERMISSION GRANTED

Give us permission to be Gentlemen Barbarians. Actually, we don't care about your permission. Jesus, by his life, has already said Permission Granted. That's good enough for us.

Permission granted for good manners, yes. Shouting

down evil, yes. Bearing arms in defense of liberty for ourselves and our posterity, yes. Tackling hard on the gridiron, yes. Loving the ideals of America, yes.

We don't care if you're redneck, white-collar, or blue blood, as long as you stand for the Red, White, and Blue.

Permission granted for sensuality and sexuality within the bounds of marriage. Yes, yes, and yes. For a sexual appetite that leads single Alphas toward marriage, yes.

Permission granted for the right to speak our mind plainly and without editing. The freedom to speak our wants. Making a ton of money. Living humbly in a modest home. Studying war. Unleashing the warrior within when called for. Building a home. Leading a quiet and respectable life. There is nothing here that Scripture doesn't already endorse.

It's time for the church to wipe away its perpetual frown of disapproval at traditional masculinity. It's time for the church to repent of the platonic body/spirit dualism that turned us into wussified messes in the first place. The body is good. The material realm is good. God made it. He called it good. We agree.

Alpha Christians are gentlemen. We have good manners. We are considerate of those around us. We stand to give grandma a seat. And the only thing that would ever keep us from standing for our flag is physical disability. We love our wives, we love our kids, we love the church, and we love the world for whom Christ died. We seek to elevate ourselves socially, intellectually, financially, and spiritually, but not at the expense of others. We want to live and let live. We tell the truth, tempered with love.

Alpha Christians are also barbarians. We crap and piss and sweat and stink and fight and snore and yell. We protect the vulnerable, using our bodies as shields if need be. We fight back the forces of darkness, using whatever righteous power is required. We tell stupid jokes. We get too loud. We thrive on adrenaline. And as Christ loved the church and gave himself up for it, we stand ready to do the same. You're welcome.

If churches won't respect us as we are, don't expect us to show up at your next pointless get-together.

But if you make a place for us at the table, we will show up. And when the devil comes calling—as a thug to break your windows, or as a legalist to judge your worship team, or as a bureaucrat promising "how much she cares"—we'll step up for you, and you'll be glad we're here.

FREE WILL_

Is life so dear, or peace so sweet, as to be purchased at
the price of chains and slavery? Forbid it, Almighty
God! I know not what course others may take; but as
for me, give me liberty or give me death!
~*Patrick Henry*

So, attend carefully to your posture. Quit drooping and
hunching around. Speak your mind. Put your desires
forward, as if you had a right to them—at least the same
right as others. Walk tall and gaze forthrightly ahead.
Dare to be dangerous.
~*Jordan B. Peterson*

ALPHA CHRISTIANS DON'T LIKE BEING TOLD what
we can and can't do.

God created humans in his own image. Whatever
else this means, it means that God sliced off human-

sized slivers of some of his own attributes and implanted them in our deepest being.

Beating deep within the breast of every Alpha Christian is a determined, driven, undeniable measure of God-given sovereignty.

Alphas are the captains of their ship, the pilots of their lives, and the masters of their domain. God gave us dominion and commanded us to use it. This is the essence of free will.

Ever since the Fall, humans have either been abusing free will or shrinking back from it. In that Fall, the human will fell into bondage to sin and Satan.

But in redemption, Christ has restored us to the throne of our lives. Paul says that Christians "reign in life" and Alpha Christians take him up on that (Romans 5:17).

In theology, it's called free will. In history, the founders of America called it liberty.

We believe in liberty because God gave us free will.

Free will means that as Alphas we choose the course of our lives. No person, government, boss, demon, nanny state, bureaucrat, pastor, priest, pope, or church has any business coercing us into anything.

Yes, we obey the laws when they are lawful. Yes, we respect our neighbors. We respect the authority of teachers in classrooms, police officers doing their duty, and any other legitimately constituted authority. We practice self-sacrifice to bless those within our realm.

But we do these things as disparate acts of free will, not because we've been cowed into submission.

We are submitted, but not submissive. We may be pliant, but never compliant. If we listen to you, it is because we choose to, not because we have to. Even our acquiescence is an exercise of sovereign choice.

WHAT FREE WILL MEANS FOR GOD'S PEOPLE

For a genuinely saved Christian...

Free will means that tyranny has its source in Satan, no matter how well-intentioned its advocates may be.

Free will means that Alphas take complete responsibility for the quality of their lives. No excuses. No one to blame. No whining. No entitlement.

Free will requires both risk and reward. Alpha Christians recognize life without a safety net as part of character development.

Free will means recognizing the evils that have been perpetrated against us, along with the determination to rise above a mindset of victimhood. We are not to blame for the wounds that others have inflicted upon us. We do, however, take responsibility for rising above those wounds, without letting them dominate our lives. We can do all things through Christ, who gives us strength.

Free will means that Alphas never put their hands in another person's pocket. They never live by the sweat of another person's brow. They resist the tyranny that justifies taking from one to give to another, without the consent of the governed. They resent the theft of wealth from generations not yet born through unsustainable deficit spending—it is truly taxation without representation. They hate the lazy, spoiled cowards who blackmail the populace with threats of violence for their own financial, political, and narcissistic gain. They believe that if an able-bodied, able-minded man will not work, he should not eat. They oppose powerful corporations that abuse power to suffocate competition.

Free will means that Alphas live and let live. Your realm is your realm. Your property is your property. Your lifestyle is your business. I will pitch in and help wherever I am asked. But otherwise, I'll leave you alone and I expect the same from you. Actually, I demand the same from you. Don't tread on me.

Free will means that Alphas will never domineer, coerce, subjugate or in any way trample the liberty of women, men, children, or anyone. We respect each person's dominion and right to self-determination. We devote ourselves to creating spaces where our family members can thrive, expressing their truest selves according to each one's God-given callings.

Free will exalts the individual over the collective.

Free will means that government must be kept in check, as the most dangerous force on earth is political operatives who usurp the place of God.

Free will means we don't want your utopia. We'll wait for the one Jesus establishes when he returns. Anything else can be only well-intentioned, freedom-hating Luciferianism.

Free will requires free-enterprise market economies and property rights. No man works to serve the collective.

Free will exalts liberty above security. Give me liberty or give me death.

Free will recognizes a man's home is his castle, knowing no castle can stand unless it can be defended with force.

Free will means Alpha Christians do not need elites, experts, Brights, or any other self-appointed Messiahs to tell us what to do. We know what's best for us and for our families, so best you keep your opinion to yourself.

Free will is the supreme divine institution created by God for the human race. Every other institution was created to protect, defend, strengthen, and bless human free will.

Before Christ enters our lives, the human will is in bondage, shackled to Satan and dead in trespasses and sins. This is the acid spit of hell, making our world so brutal and cruel.

But to believe in Christ crucified and risen again, and to receive his salvation, and to know his truth is to be set free once for all.

When the framers of the Declaration of Independence, the Constitution, and the Bill of Rights penned their immortal words, they did so with profound reverence for free will, which they called liberty. They viewed government as liberty's gravest threat. They knew government would be run by morally fallen people, so they invented limited government to protect us from their abuse. They learned these truths from the Bible. Alpha Christians stand with them and always will.

WE BAND OF BROTHERS_

> We few, we happy few, we band of
>   brothers;
> For he to-day that sheds his blood
>   with me
> Shall be my brother; be he ne'er so vile,
> This day shall gentle his condition:
> And gentlemen in England now a-bed
> Shall think themselves accursed they
>   were not here,
> And hold their manhoods cheap whiles
>   any speaks
> That fought with us upon Saint
>   Crispin's day.

- SHAKESPEARE, HENRY V

To MODERNIZE KING HENRY V, like it or not, the battle is upon us. If you plan to sit it out, just shred your man card now. Slink over there to the corner and join "those cold and timid souls who know neither victory nor defeat." While you're at it, get yourself a new pronoun. Your incessant hand wringing and endless talk will bring us down. We Alpha Christians have a war to fight. Go calm your jittery nerves with the rest of the Betas.

But we have several problems with this war.

One is that we are decent human beings. We're not about to take to the streets and riot. That's against our moral code. We'll leave that for the spoiled rich kids and for the professional thugs who leech off of their parents and neighbors.

Another problem is that we have jobs and families. Alpha Christians are productive members of society. When do we have time to picket, demonstrate, riot, or join protest movements?

Furthermore, we are not about violence. We are not about to take up arms. We repudiate violence, except in defense of ourselves and others under threat of immediate harm.

But we can and will act. Now is the time.

The forces of decency have always assumed that when the forces of darkness finally push too fast, too far, there would be such a backlash that they wouldn't get away with it.

It's time to check that assumption.

HOW FAR CAN SATAN PUSH?

Who's winning today's culture war? How much assault can our society take?

Was the judicial decision to ratify gay marriage too fast, too far?

Was the locking down of our country and the muzzling of our populace too fast, too far?

How about burly men competing in women's sports or naked dudes prancing around our daughters' locker rooms? What about Drag Queen story time in public libraries? What about the US military paying for transgender surgeries? What about the rising movement to legitimize pedo sex with children?

Even the devil is shocked he has gotten away with as much as he has, as fast as he has.

It's not enough when our society saw professional athletes blatantly disrespecting the American flag. It's not enough that every news story in the media elite marches in lockstep with the same narrative being pushed by Hollywood, social media, big government socialists, and academia—a narrative that tolerates every aberrant view and suppresses traditional values, Christianity, and any idea of American exceptionalism. It's not enough that even our language is hijacked, and words redefined, and symbols of patriotic honor reviled as emblems of hate.

Culture is too distracted to care. But does the church care?

What about Bibles and Christian groups banned in public schools while every sexual deviancy gets a fully funded club? What about Christian campuses —"gospel-centered" universities—with officially sanctioned LGBTQ organizations? What about professors who openly mock Christianity? What about tax dollars being used to fund high school classes in "porn literacy"?[1]

Does today's typical American care? Do they even notice? Do everyday Christians care? Our society comments on social media, then gripes, then yawns, and moves on.

What do Christians say about churches and pastors that have replaced evangelism with social action, worship with trance-inducing repetition, and Scripture with political theory, meaningless fluff, and new revelations from self-appointed apostles? The Old Rugged Cross is forgotten, the offense of sin is erased, hell is emptied, love wins, and an inoffensive Jesus nurtures a global Church of Nice. Evangelism has virtually died. What will we tell our grandchildren we were doing when Christianity disappeared from the land?

Alpha Christians will tell them we took action. We will tell them we fought the good fight and paid a price to do it.

Maybe American society was pushed too far when riots broke out in American cities across the land. When we saw nightly images of fires, looting, and worse. When there were videos of open violence, gun-toting thugs terrorizing the streets, and reports of rape. That would push us into action, no doubt. Surely that would cause District Attorneys across the land to at least arrest these monsters and press charges. But it didn't. There's something dramatically wrong with our beloved country.

What about desecrating the sacred monuments to revered heroes of our history? Not enough yet? Then what about establishing a new nation within the borders of an American city? What about foreign interference in our elections? What about the weaponization of climate change, the theft of intellectual property by state-sponsored actors, and the utter blindness of a society so anesthetized by pleasure or opioids they hardly blink an eye? Surely our officials will never let it get that far! Surely there will be a swift and fierce response at the national level!

The devil is laughing—and he's just getting warmed up.

What was unthinkable yesterday is not only normalized today, it is called a sacrament by those who believe nothing is sacred but their own abominations.

This makes us wonder, *what is unthinkable today?* The perversions and desecrations we think could never happen are already bullet points on the power-brokers' agenda. Count on it.

The trampling of freedoms, the meteoric rise of big government socialism, the infiltration of Marxism into every major institution, the war on Christians, the centralization of power at the top, and the economic enslavement of our nation and our nation's children through debt—the agenda marches on and anyone who would raise their voice against it barely makes a difference.

Our culture scarcely notices. But Alpha Christians won't stand for it.

GOLIATH, MEET DAVID

Goliath challenged the armies of God's people for 40 days and 40 nights, twice a day, without response. Eighty challenges. Eighty invitations to man-to-man combat. Eighty threats of enslavement.

For 40 days and nights, the giant went unanswered.

On day 41, a teenage Alpha showed up. His name was David. He was a blue-collar worker. A loner. An outsider, even to his own family. David heard Goliath's challenge only once and declared *Enough!*

He looked around only to see his brothers and their wussified comrades hiding in their tents, wringing their Beta hands, and trying to figure out what to do. Some called for more analysis. Some said the situation was hopeless.

David was shocked, not so much at the giant's challenge, but at the utter lack of response by God's own people.

He had only one question.

"Who is this uncircumcised Philistine that he should defy the armies of the living God" (1 Samuel 17:26)?

To call him uncircumcised was to call him secular, godless, and profane.

To call him a Philistine was to call him defiant against the One True God and, therefore, under a divine curse.

The Enemy has not changed. Goliath stands for every force in every age that stands for secularism and profanity and that has arrayed itself against heaven, daring God to hurl down his curse.

David knew his enemy, and Alphas do too.

Our enemies are every dark force hellbent on shoving secularism, godlessness, and profanity down our cultural throat.

Our enemies are those who bow before grotesque idols. Those who would enslave us and our children.

Our enemies are the satanic cults of big-government socialism and secularism, bent on destroying America and liberty because they must wipe them out first if they expect to wipe Christians off the face of the earth.

Goliath is still bullying the world, and his challenge remains largely unanswered.

But Alpha Christians know a secret. Walking in Christ, we are the armies of the Living God. Armed with the Sacred Scriptures, we are invincible.

Who are these uncircumcised Philistines that they should defy the armies of the Living God?

Alpha Christians will not shiver in our tents. We will not run from this fight. That day has passed. The night is fast approaching. We put on the armor of light, and we take our stand for Christ and his Everlasting Gospel.

THE TRIUMPH OF THE CRUCIFIED ONE

Everyone who claims Jesus Christ as Savior has been enlisted in His cosmic army of grace and truth. We are born again into the army of God.

Alpha Christians leap headlong into the fray. With grit and grace, we face the foe.

We do not shrink from this unceasing battle of the ages. It is a cosmic conflict between God and Satan, truth and deception, life and death, heaven and hell. Satan is expending his final putrid breaths—the principalities and powers are raging against the gospel of God.

Every day, new Goliaths strut the earth, spitting their threats, and intimidating the Betas.

But God has his warriors. We are here, Alpha Christians, standing in the shadow of the Cross.

While others have swallowed the devil's lies, Alphas stand on the unchanging truth of an unchanging Bible.

While others must calm their nerves in the Church of Nice, Alphas have made ready for war.

While others seek compromise and peace with God-hating, church-destroying, demon-believing Philistines, Alphas sing *Onward Christian Soldiers* and march into the fray.

While others whine for unity, Alphas stand for a truth so true it makes every man a liar.

While others connive to make a bloodied Savior dignified, we proclaim to all who will hear "the offense of the Cross" with no apologies.

While others justify riots, spout critical race theory, and crawl into their safe spaces, Alphas stand in the crossfire of propaganda and lies, upholding the sanctity of life and the truth of the inerrant Word of God.

While others have erased hell and declared "love wins," Alphas stand in awe of the dreadful wrath of God, declaring love can't win if divine justice loses.

While others waste the church's time and money saving society and whitewashing the devil's world, Alphas are willing to spend and be spent to save souls from eternal damnation. God forbid we should glory, save in the Cross.

While others self-righteously dismantle the greatest country in the history of the world, Alpha Christians remain unashamed, flag-waving patriots.

While others worship the collective, Alphas stand

with the individual—the locus of free will and human dominion in God's grand plan.

We are Alpha Christians. Deal with us. We won't go away.

Yes, there are times when Alphas grow weary and weak, broken and tired. There are times when we do not feel like the triumphant army of the Living God.

But when the night is darkest, and when fear rises in our throats, Alphas lean into the fray. We fight the good fight of faith. We endure hardship. We speak the truth in tough love. As soldiers of Christ, we arise.

The battle is on. The weapons of our warfare are mighty through God. He is the Champion we need in the fight for our lives.

No one can stay His hand.

Nothing can thwart His will.

Nobody can defeat His purposes.

No force can shake His throne.

Heaven is not afraid.

God is not dismayed.

Satan is a defeated foe.

We follow the Unconquerable Warrior. We ride with the King of kings and Lord of lords. We stand with the one who defeated sin, shattered the gates of hell, crushed the head of Satan, and sent the armies of darkness scurrying right off the cliff into the seething lake of fire.

We shout to the world the Triumph of the Crucified One.

Alpha Christians are not intimidated by the giants on the horizon.

We won't back down.

We won't give in.

We won't wimp out.

We won't compromise.

We are marching from faith to faith, from victory to victory, and from glory to glory.

Call us fools. Call us haters. Call us dangerous. Marginalize us. Cancel us. Redefine us. Label us.

Alpha Christians are bloodied but unbowed. We take our marching orders from God above, and he alone —not the tyrants of the earth—tells us who we are.

The victory is won. The celebration is coming. We already see with the eyes of faith that glorious day when God has the last laugh, when the false prophets tumble headlong into perdition, when the tyrants choke on their impotence, and when a humiliated devil is shown to be the weakling liar he always was.

Alpha Christians are the Overcomers.

Alphas see the day coming when the God of peace will crush Satan under our feet—meaning Alpha Christians' feet—shortly.

Alphas see the day when every knee shall bow and tongue confess that Jesus Christ is Lord to the glory of God the Father. What a day that will be! What a wonder! What a triumph! What a spectacle to dazzle the angels and to rout the demonic hordes.

And in those darkest moments, when the devil seems ascendant, and hope is almost lost, Alphas listen closely with the ears of faith —

> *And when the fight*
> *Is fierce, the warfare long*
> *Steals on the ear*
> *The distant triumph song.*
> *And hearts are brave*
> *Again and hearts are strong.*
> *Alleluia.*
> *Alleluia.*

- C.H. MORRIS, 1905

By faith, we hear the shouts of victory from ten thousand times ten thousand fellow soldiers of the Cross—men and women, the saints of God—valiant warriors who have entered heaven before us.

Today, the battle is on. Alpha Christians take up the whole armor of God. We are armed for this fight. We march forth in the steps of the Invincible, All-conquering, Triumphant, Ascendant, Reigning, King of kings and Lord of lords.

When the kings of the earth conspire together with the principalities and powers of hell to throw off the rule of God and of his Christ, He who sits in heaven shall laugh. The Omnipotent One has nothing to fear.

Who are these secularized termites to stand against the armies of the living God?

Alpha Christians stand with him and he stands with us.

The fight is on.

Come join us.

Let's watch some giants fall.

TAKE ACTION_

Some wish to live within the sound
Of church or chapel bell.
I want to run a rescue shop
Within a yard of hell.
~*C.T. Studd*

Deep in his heart, every man longs for a battle to fight,
an adventure to live, and a beauty to rescue. ~*John
Eldredge*

DAVID PICKED up five smooth stones. It took only one to slay Goliath. We've collected fifty smooth stones here for Alpha Christians. Pick up a few and see what happens. We maintain this list along with links and more information on our website at AlphaChristians.org.

1. Get up, read the Bible, say a prayer every day.

2. Sign the Alpha Christian Manifesto. Visit AlphaChristians.org.

3. Join (or start) an Alpha Christians chapter. Spread the word. Share this book.

4. Volunteer to be a Judge of Election.

5. Volunteer to be a Poll Watcher.

6. Run for a local school board. Represent your people and vote your conscience. If you can't run, at least show up for their meetings and speak up for reality. Be respectful; don't make it personal.

7. Run for a seat on your county Board of Supervisors or City Council.

8. Read a book about marriage and family. Invite your wife and kids to read along.

9. Take your family to church. Don't skip.

10. Write a book.

11. Take a class in music or art at a community college. Join a local band/orchestra/opera.

12. Register to vote. Vote.

13. Start a side hustle. Be an entrepreneur. Create some jobs.

14. Donate to your church. If you already give, boost it.

15. Take your son fishing or to a concert. Bring one of his friends.

16. Take your daughter fishing or to a concert.

Bring one of her friends.

17. Date your wife.

18. If you're single, start dating Christian women without having sex. Find a good woman and marry her.

19. Take a dance class.

20. Take up woodworking. Build a grandfather clock or a dining room table and chairs.

21. Volunteer to care for babies at your church.

22. Start attending Celebrate Recovery or another recovery group.

23. Volunteer for Little League in any sport.

24. Join the Strenuous Life (artofmanliness.com)

25. Volunteer in the public school.

26. Volunteer in your local mission.

27. Quit mainstream social media.

28. Quit porn. Focus your sexual energy on your wife. Get help if needed.

29. Sing the National Anthem, loud and proud.

30. Volunteer at a Veterans Home.

31. Take a course in Apologetics.

32. Sign up for Theological School. (Visit VeritasSchool.life for a realistic option run by me.) Lead a small group or Sunday School class.

33. Learn how to shoot a gun.

34. Take up archery or martial arts, or both.

35. Go skeet shooting, take your family.

36. Homeschool your kids or put them into a Christian school.

37. Drive your kids to church, youth groups, Awana, and kids' clubs.

38. Routinely patronize a few mom-and-pop shops.

39. Take care of your home. Upgrade your neighborhood.

40. Get out of debt.

41. Get healthy.

42. Buy books from a local bookstore instead of online.

43. Control your sex life. Enjoy your sex life.

44. Keep politics out of family get-togethers. The family bond is more important.

45. Speak up against totalitarianism in the right places at the right times.

46. Mentor young people.

47. Write a note of support to your pastor in October (Pastor Appreciation Month).

48. Buy a good leather Bible for every person in your family. Write a nice note inside the front cover. Read the Christmas accounts from it before you open presents.

49. Memorize one Bible verse per week. Don't worry if you forget them as you go.

50. Tell your lost friends about Jesus, even if you don't feel worthy.

GET INVOLVED_

Visit AlphaChristians.org to get involved. Read our Articles. Study the Bible with us. Launch an Alpha Christians chapter.

———

Bring an Alpha Christians event to your community or church—Email bookings@AlphaChristians.org

———

To go deeper into problems plaguing today's church, read Bill Giovannetti's book
Chaos: As Goes the Church So Goes the World

———

You can support the cause by buying Alpha Christians apparel, caps, and other merchandise at AlphaChristians.org.

Go deeper into God's Word than ever before with Veritas School of Biblical Ministry—an online, work-at-your-own-pace, super affordable Theology School for Everyday Christians, at VeritasSchool.life. Look in the FAQs for a discounted tuition for readers of *Alpha Christians*.

5. THE CONSPIRACY

1. From BBC News, June 21, 2020 at https://www.bbc.com/news/world-asia-57549653 retrieved October 11, 2021.

6. THE GENTLEMAN BARBARIAN

1. Worth reading. David Murrow. *Why Men Hate Going to Church* (Nashville: Thomas Nelson, 2005).
2. Amy Lorin, "What Is Toxic Masculinity" in Very Well Mind, 2020 at https://www.verywellmind.com/what-is-toxic-masculinity-5075107 retrieved July 2021.
3. Ibid.

8. WE BAND OF BROTHERS

1. The story is here: https://www.audacy.com/knx1070/articles/cbs-news/boston-program-teaching-porn-literacy-in-high-schools.

Made in the USA
Monee, IL
06 November 2021